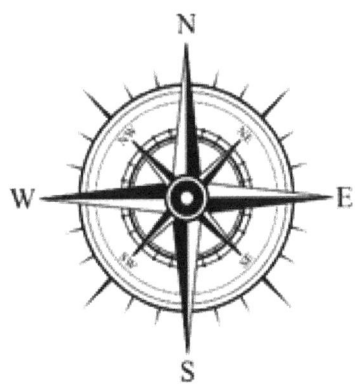

"-NEXT-"

NAVIGATING THE SEASONS, SETBACKS AND SYSTEMS IN LIFE

DR. RONALD K. THORNHILL, SR.

Published by

LEZEAL Enterprises, LLC

P.O. Box 252, Lawrenceville, Virginia 23868

Copyright © 2024 by Dr. Ronald K. Thornhill, Sr.

All rights reserved. No part of this book may be reproduced, stored in a retrieval system, or transmitted in any form by any means electronic, mechanical, photocopying, recording or otherwise without written permission of the publisher, except for the inclusion of brief quotations in a review.

ISBN 979-8-218-40842-8

Disclaimer: Although the author/publisher has made every effort to ensure that the information in this book was correct at press time and while this publication is designed to provide accurate information in regard to the subject matter covered, the author/publisher assumes no responsibility for errors, inaccuracies, omissions, or any other inconsistencies herein and hereby disclaim any liability to any party for any loss, damage, or disruption caused by errors or omissions, whether such errors or omissions result from negligence, accident, or any other cause. This publication is meant as a source of valuable information for the reader, however, it is not meant as a substitute for direct expert assistance. If such a level of assistance is required, the services of a competent professional should be sought.

ISBN: 979-8-218-40842-8

Praise for
"NEXT"

As a Life Coach, often I am referred to as "The Nudger" for my ability to gently guide my clients through their journey of seeking and exploring.

In this book, Dr. Thornhill rips the Band-Aid off the notion that Christians are exempt from the happenstances of life. In fact, the book gives Christians everywhere permission to put themselves first and it is packed with tools to show them how to navigate their journey of self-awareness.

Dr. Thornhill possesses the innate ability to captivate readers from all walks of life by sharing his life hiccups and hard conversations that pushed him toward his next.

To the reader, this book is filled with life nuggets that will lend to your growth spiritually, emotionally, and mentally. If you desire change, are stuck, or are ready to see what else life has to offer, Congratulations! Take a chance on yourself. Dr. Thornhill wrote this book specifically for you!

-Gigi Hopkins
MSN.Ed, BSN, RN, CDP, CLC
Clinical Educator/ Certified Life Coach

As Superintendent of many schools in rural North Carolina, I have had the privilege of watching students grow and move to their next phase in life. However, it is never easy going into a school to let the principal or school administrator know that their tenure is up, or it is time to move on. Change is the necessary ingredient in any district if we want the school division to grow and move to the next level. Dr. Thornhill, in his book *"Next"*, does a masterful job in walking the reader through those tough steps to get to their *"next"* after a mini-setback or a major shift in life.

It is a very practical guide, but challenging read if we want to continuously change and push ourselves to the next level of growth, achievement, and leadership. His words, wisdom, and life nuggets will grab and hold your attention throughout each chapter.

Much of the advice given is very much aligned to my thought processes and how I attempt to lead and inspire others in my organization every day. While data may drive instruction, the willingness to change and look through a different set of lenses each day, not only helps the learner, but the teacher as well. I strongly encourage educators and practitioners to pick up a copy of this book to add to your tool chest. It just may be the read to push you into your "next."

Otis Smallwood
Superintendent, Bertie County Schools

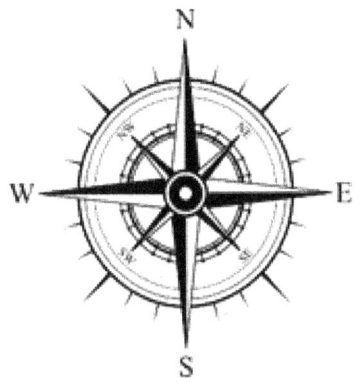

"-NEXT-"

Navigating the Seasons, Setbacks and Systems in life

DR. RONALD K. THORNHILL, SR.

DEDICATION

To Trice, my wife, my greatest supporter in every venture and all that I have ever sought out to do. In tough times and in good times, you have epitomized those words and what it really means for better or for worse. Thanks for sticking with me and loving me even when I did not love myself. Love you much.

To my children, Ashley and Ronald and even my grandson Josh, I love you all so much for being all you can be and trusting the process even when the process sometimes did not make sense or got cloudy along the way.

Finally, to my grandmother and mother, you both are gone but never forgotten! I am what I am and who I am today because of you.

Love you both!

Table of Contents

Foreword 11

Introduction 13

Chapter 1: The Blueprint 19
    Unpacking the Blueprint in Relationships   20
    Unpacking the Blueprint of Change   22
    Unpacking the Fears in Life   23

Chapter 2: The Battle Plan 25

Chapter 3: The Basics 33
    Unpacking your Purpose   34
    Unpacking your Passion   35
    Unpacking the Process   36

Chapter 4 : The Transition 39
    Unpacking Turning Points   40
    Unpacking Lasting Points   41

Chapter 5: The Transaction 43
    Unpacking the deception   44
    Unpacking the real deal   45

Chapter 6 : The Transformation 47
    Unpacking the Shock   48
    Unpacking the Shame   49

Chapter 7: The Failure 51
    Unpacking Scars that Remind Us But Do Not Define Us   52

Unpacking the Scars to be a Better Person 53
Unpacking the Scars to Find Your Purpose 55

Chapter 8: The Faith 57
Unpacking the Fear that Blocks our Faith 58
Unpacking the Fight For Our Faith 59
Unpacking the Multiple Lens of Faith 60

Chapter 9: The Follow-Up 63
Unpacking the Growing Pains 65
Unpacking the Changes, We Cannot Control 66
Unpacking How to Move In Silence 67

Chapter 10: The Call 69
Unpacking the Pitfalls Behind The Call 71
Unpacking the Detours Behind The Call 72
Unpacking the Pain Behind The Call 73

Chapter 11: The Commitment 75
Unpacking the Cost Behind Our Commitment 77
Unpacking the Purpose Behind Our Commitment 78
Unpacking Quality Relationships Behind Our Commitment 79

Chapter 12: The Commission 81
Unpacking the Next Season 82
Unpacking the Setbacks/Setups 83
Unpacking the Systems 85

About the Author 88

FOREWORD

This book by Dr. Ronald K. Thornhill is a gift to its readers, and those who are concerned with the welfare of this country. Dr. Thornhill, like a capable doctor, diagnosing the problem, and in a skillful manner directs his readers to the solutions.

He does so in love, with a spirit of up building. This is a fantastically courageous book, and it will single-handedly shift the conversation, anchoring spiritual doctrines, and not falling prey to sociological sayings.

We need a GPS for our personal, family, and organizational security to assist in decision-making, stress-related situations, and generational role modeling now, and in the future. Now is the time to adhere to sound principles and high standards to make maximum use of our Life's Journey. An old adage "failure to prepare is preparing to fail"!

Ronald Keith Thornhill outlines not only the methodology for success, but also its principles and practices visionaries have suggested through the years. His analogies, reasoning, and steps are clearly outlined in simple terms, as to allow the reader full insight to fulfilling results. Prepare yourself and others for an exciting thought provoking read.

~George B. Lancaster
Educator, Counselor, Legendary Coach for over 50 years,
member of five Hall of Fames

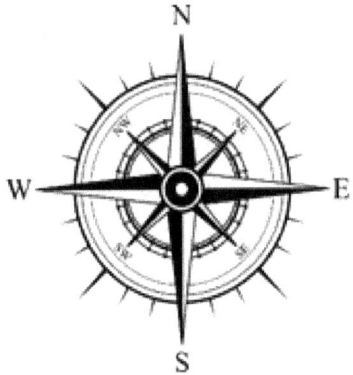

Introduction

I can remember growing up in the City of Richmond, Virginia playing basketball at Maymont Playground. Some days we would be on the court all day; until someone beat us, and we would immediately say NEXT, signifying we got the next game! So, who was it that ended your winning streak? Who is your next opponent? What is your next step in life…what does your next season hold? How do you bounce back from a setback? How do you recover from a game-changing surgery? I hope this book will serve as a springboard to your finding meaningful solutions to these questions!

One of the hardest things to do in life is moving on or moving into the next season of our lives; especially, after an unexpected setback or systems that are put in place that ultimately work against us. Moreover, it is not always easy because of the uncertainties, the challenges that may lie in front of us. Many times, what pushes us into our next phase or stage in life is someone who cares and is willing to call us on the carpet. What are you saying, Pastor? Sometimes it takes those closest to us, and those who probably know us better than most to call us out, but when we are, it is ultimately the setup for transitioning into our "Next"! It pushes us or transitions us into the next phase or stage of our lives. This has prompted me to pen these words, so what is next?

Recently, I had a candid conversation with someone I admire dearly, and she actually called me out. Prior to the conversation, I asked her if it was good or bad, and she said it depends on how you take it! She had a mouthful for me. While it was not pleasant to hear these "truths" and "revelations," I had to do one of two things, embrace the truth (because she definitely read my mail and was spot on) or continue to wear the mask because it was convenient; not because of COVID, but because I was comfortable! What is so annoying and, yet, amazing is that I knew it was the truth, and I was tired of wearing the mask! I had some ways about me that were not pleasant, as we all do, but I had become so comfortable with who I was that I forgot about who I had become. So now I have come to a place and space in my life where I must ask the question am I ready for "my next," or do I continue to be who I am. Satisfying those who think they know me and, at the same time, never becoming who I was created to be. Thus, becoming like so many with incredible potential but never reaching their ultimate destiny in life. Perhaps you are in the same situation wrestling with that formidable opponent "self," waiting for that conversation or confrontation with that person bold enough to catch us at the right moment to "Call us Out."

In an ever-changing landscape called life, sometimes we need to hear it from someone else; you are not in it alone, and "this too shall pass." "Navigating the seasons, setbacks, and systems" provides a three-point approach to help you walk through the daily struggles that come with each day that passes. We all have those challenges, battles, and, even at times, adversities that hit us unexpectedly. However, navigating through them with minimal damage can be the difference between life and death, remaining sane or insane, or just simply living, for that matter. Moreover, life has an uncanny way of unraveling if we do not have mechanisms and systems in place to keep us grounded. Having recently published my first book, "Menspiration," along with the workbook, I still have so much more to say. Particularly as it relates to family and navigating through this changing culture.

It is always helpful to have access to a GPS to get you through those tough spots when you feel that you have lost your way, made a wrong turn, or simply felt stuck because of a bad decision in life. One of the greatest misnomers in life is that it is a sign of weakness to ask for help. The truth of the matter is that we either have all been there or have felt too embarrassed to admit that we were the ones who needed help. Even though they have passed the bar, every successful attorney consults the "Precedent Decision Manual" to determine if there is a case they may be unfamiliar with and need additional assistance. Every teacher consults the "Manual of Best Practices" if an area within their subject matter is unclear or need further explanation. All doctors are "practicing physicians" because there are areas within their profession they may not be up to the most current medical practices. Therefore, if these professions recognize the need for additional assistance, we can seek additional assistance if we are unsure.

For so long, we have bought into the notion, that if you been doing something for so long, you should have mastered it with no further questions. Because of this thinking, many of us shortchange others and ourselves by not continuing to ask those age-old questions, "So how did you accomplish your success" or "How did you get through that storm or setback." While all of our situations are different and unique to our individual context, there is still much to learn and many to benefit from a "simple how to." It is upon this premise that we journey together to find "Nuggets to Navigate" the Seasons, Setbacks, and Systems" in life. We often think it is over when we encounter those pitfalls, potholes, or dead ends in life. However, the key to bouncing back, building a new team of players, and simply believing, again, is to push through the pain, be patient during the process and be persistent about the promise.

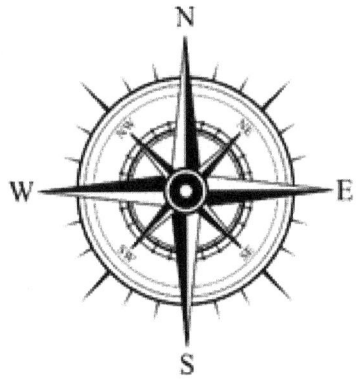

Chapter 1

The Blueprint

Growing up in the city of Richmond, it was always fun to watch new homes built because, as kids, we would run through them and always try to figure out why the pipes were all over the place, the rooms did not have doors on them, and other items seemed as though they were out of place. However, one day as we were playing, we found a drawing with white lines and a blue background, and of course, none of us knew what it was. We later discovered the Blueprint laid out the design of the house. Although we could not read it, we figured out the house was according to the picture or design. Often in life, we may stumble across pictures, drawings, and even designs that may seem unclear at the time, but as time passes and we move through the different chapters in life, the pictures begin to take form and serve to frame a larger narrative in our lives. Although the Blueprint gives us a detailed picture of what is coming, the challenge for many of us is moving to the "Next" phase of the drawing and bringing the project closer to fruition. In essence, the Blueprint gives us the framework of what is to become, but we still have to make it happen by taking the next steps in the process. So how do we take the drawings of where we are in life and transition to our "Next"? Our "Next" will differ for each of us because we are all at different phases, stages, and chapters in life; however, the steps to move forward in the process are transferrable. Many times, we have the idea, vision, or blueprint, but the challenge is giving voice to that vision and putting some meat on those dry bones! So let us buckle up and journey together to put some meat on our "Next" bones!

Unpacking the Blueprint in Relationships

With any blueprint, it is critical that one understands that it is a two-dimensional set of drawings provides a detailed visual representation of how an architect want the building to look. Blueprints typically specify a building's dimensions, construction materials, and the exact placement of all its components. With that said, let us unpack the blueprint of relationships. Especially since that is the cornerstone of us moving forward or the mud that keeps us stuck in a ditch. By no means do I proclaim to be a guru on relationships, but if your relationship with your mother or father is not the best, it will definitely affect how you move forward in any relationship in general. I will never forget how I would often say I would never be like my father because he always worked hard, and provided for Mom and my siblings, but he never was an affectionate Dad. In fact, I never saw him kiss or hug my Mom. Even today, I am not that affectionate when it comes to my family. It is amazing how we become more like our parents than we ever thought! Therefore, as we continue to unpack this blueprint of relationships, we must become intentional about what we want similar to a detailed drawing of everything we want in a building. Some may think it is farfetched to have high standards, but as some often say, "If you don't stand for something, you will fall for anything." Do not let standards be too low and then get upset when they turn out to be what you thought…. "Low Down, dirty dog," do not blame the dog; blame the one who offered the dog the bones. Moreover, if you do not know what you want, you will always end up with someone who is a placeholder instead of a heart giver, who gives from the heart at the start. Do not forget, you are the architect, so it is critical that you know how to read the drawings, so you know what to expect in your next chapter regarding relationships.

Unpacking the Blueprint of Change

Change is one of the most challenging things to unpack primarily because it consists of many moving parts and is perhaps the most uncomfortable. However, if handled correctly, it can yield tremendous dividends. Those who have learned to navigate the pitfalls and process of change are more likely to succeed. Change can range from the death of a loved one, divorce or separation, change in job or career, health, and so many more. All these changes can have a permanent effect on all involved. There are three keys to successfully navigating change: Face it head-on, and do not run from it. By running away from change, we will never realize the potential within us that will only come out of us when pushed to change. This book is the product of being pushed to do, be, and expect better. Thus, making others around me better, started with facing the music of change head-on. Amazingly, our destiny is the process of change. Secondly, we must embrace change by accepting it and not fighting it. This is difficult for so many because a certain level of discomfort and uncertainty comes with change. The "fight or flight" mentality immediately comes in. Embracing it means I will "ride this wave," regardless of how high or rough the waters may be. Ultimately, when we embrace it, we then become *"the change we want to see in others"* (Ghandi)

Thirdly, we navigate change by shaping the narrative. Too often, we allow others to write and coop our stories, especially after a tragedy or life-changing event. For example, when I experienced a tragedy early in life with my brother killing another young man because of bullying. I could have gone into depression because everyone watched us to see how we would respond – not knowing that at an early age of 12, the trauma from that incident could affect not only my brother, but my entire family. Furthermore, not having experience in counseling, or anyone to help get us through, made it twice as bad. Looking back, I now realize that getting help would help shape my own narrative versus buying into what society and data says about trauma, tragedy, and the long-term effects of no treatment at all. However, having support from others always serves as a deterrent from further emotional pain and ultimately helps to shape our own narrative from life-changing events.

Unpacking the Fears in Life

Fear is a quiet killer. It kills dreams, visions, and many who are on their way to greatness! It backs us into a corner, paralyzes our potential, debilitates our destiny, and annihilates our ambitions. As a result, it is the ultimate game changer. The sad commentary is that allowing fear to change who we are will change where we are going! Setbacks sometimes will cause fear to spring up, and many times, it becomes hard to navigate past it; however, I have found some simple strategies for overcoming fear. One of the first things to deal with when combating fear is overcoming our preconceived ideas or opinions about people we do not know. For example, when I was growing up, my family always had issues with a certain family in our neighborhood because they treated us differently. As I got older, I was afraid to reach out to that family because I thought they also had issues with me. As it turns out, one day, I asked the brother of one of the family members, what his issue with us was and he said nothing. He further stated that it happened with his grandparents, and never involved anyone else. Therefore, for 20 or more years, we all were afraid to talk to each other because of what happened earlier with our grandparents. Personal beliefs or judgments without facts sometimes cause us to miss an opportunity because of fear. Although it is hard not to believe our family, the sad reality is that some things you have to walk out yourself. There is hope if you rewrite your narrative and do not allow your past to paralyze you. Secondly, fear is really a game changer. It will change where we go if we allow it to change who we are. While some things are hard to refute, we must turn the pages to move into our next chapter in life. As long as we nurse the pain, rehearse it, and curse it, the Lord cannot reverse it; and, thus, disperse it! The setbacks are, at times, devastating to overcome. However, with each step forward, we make progress. Finally, overcoming fear is a process. It does not happen overnight but over time. The key is to trust the process, not rush the process.

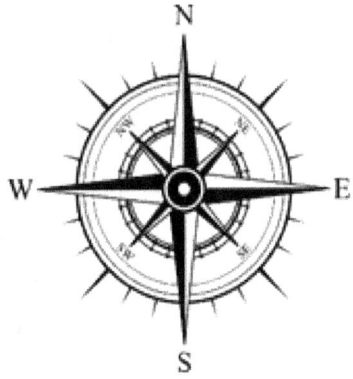

Chapter 2

The Battle Plan

One of the greatest errors we make in life is the lack of recognition that things have changed. As a result, we are battling to deal with today's problems with a yesterday's mindset. For example, if we do not recognize that things will never be as they were due to the pandemic, we are stuck as a church. If businesses do not recognize when the market shifts, they are stuck trying to handle today's challenges with yesterday's strategies. Therefore, as a church moving to a combination of in-person and virtual church helps us not just to survive but thrive. In other words, transitioning is the key to our success, and not being stuck in places. As we move from seasons and setbacks, we must examine the data and research to find out what worked and what did not work to make the necessary adjustments as we move forward. Having specific information at our disposal helps us avoid making certain mistakes twice! The relevant question for many of us is how we make the necessary adjustments when we do not realize we are stuck. How do we avoid chasing yesterday when today seems too hard to deal with? Simple, we must have a battle plan!

As most of us know, we win many of our battles in the trenches or in our minds. Those plans and places we frame early in life can determine our success later in battle. Recently, I was trying to find a frame for a picture, and I had a hard time deciding which one was the most appropriate. I asked the salesperson, and she said it is your preference, or "It's what you like". Too often, we ask others for their advice and opinions, but when they tell us what they think, sometimes, we get upset. The truth is that we all have likes and dislikes, but ultimately it is up to us to frame our world since we are responsible for paying the price for the frame. However, the key to satisfaction is making a decision that we can live with; not worrying about what others think or feel. Later, when I looked at the variety of frames the store had to offer, I realized that they had different sizes and different colors, some made out of fine wood and glass. The question then arose what was I willing to spend for the frame, and what did the picture mean to me? Certain battles in life are very similar to how we frame certain pictures. There are those precious moments that we never forget, and they almost cost us everything in life. Then, there are those times when we did not care too much about how we would frame events that take place at certain intervals in our life. After much pondering, three things stand out as it relates to how I frame my world. The price I was willing to pay, the place where I wanted to hang the picture, and the people I wanted to see the picture. Now I know some of you are probably saying, "I understand the price, but what do the place and people have to do with your frame? Well, I am glad you asked.

First, the **price** or cost is paramount to many of us because if we are not willing to pay the cost for a quality frame, the battle is greater, and then maybe what we are putting in the frame does not amount to much either. Similarly, if we do not value each day we live, we will not put the time, effort, or energy into making it the best day of our lives. We talk about "this is the day that the Lord has made, and we will rejoice in it," but one could only wonder, based on how we treat the day and sometimes others, is this really the day the Lord has made! While I am not suggesting that each day is a great or the best day, I am simply saying each day has the potential to be a great and best day if we put the time and energy into picking out the right frame for that day. Granted, with some glass frames, we risk breaking them, but each day of our lives we face situations that could break us, but that should not stop us. In addition, some are not willing to pay the price for frames, but we must remember you get what you are willing to pay for in life. However, on the other side, we cannot be upset with those who choose to pay the price for a more expensive frame, and they are delighted, excited, and rejoicing over the benefits they have received. It is not always, in what others may think or do but in how we choose to frame our individual day.

Secondly, the *place* is important because where you hang the picture constantly reminds you of what it means to you. It speaks volumes if it is the first thing you see when entering the house, if it is in the basement, in the corner, behind the curtain, that also speaks for itself. What we value will always be out front and in plain sight so that others and we can see it when they come to our home. It does not necessarily mean that nothing else matters but that this has priority.

Similarly, when we put the Lord first each day, and we speak of him to others when we are framing our day, it will also speak volumes about how and who helps frame our day. We show others that he is the priority in our life by how we frame him with others. Although we may not physically hang a picture of the Lord, when we communicate with others they can see through our actions and hear in our conversations the picture is clear and out front.

Finally, the ***people*** are important because we choose to show them who we are and whose we are suggesting that they are a part of the framing process. It is no secret that the individuals we spend the most time with daily have an impact, influence, and increase upon our daily lives. Therefore, the frame is important, but it is what we put in the frame, whom we put in it, and where we hang it. At the end of the day, others will know if this is so by how we rejoice and by whether we choose to rejoice. It is about what we make it.

Another difficulty we encounter in battle is being hungry, but never being able to satisfy those hunger pains. Moreover, being hungry but fed stale bread is just as bad. It is easy to say what we would or would not eat until we face dire circumstances or life/death situations. Looking at things in perspective, I often watch the wildlife channel and always find it amazing how those animals survive. To see a Lion or Tiger sit in the wild waiting and watching a herd of gazelles or zebras running by, trying to pick off the weakest one from the pack, and strategizing a way to kill them for their next meal. While this may sound gross and savaging, this is what happens. They wait for "fresh meat" and tear it apart as if it is their last meal.

Similarly, we also want fresh manna to survive and sustain ourselves through life's daily challenges. To get through the daily struggles, we need it each day. ***Sufficiency***, an adequate amount to meet our needs; ***Serenity***, bringing peace in every part of this troublesome world; and finally, **Security**, the state of being free from danger or threats, fills this manna.

Sufficiency is vital because, we often struggle with the notion that we do not or will not have enough to meet our daily needs. It is incredible how many of us live from paycheck to paycheck not realizing that it is similar to living from faith to faith. Now let me qualify that because I hear the bishops, pastors, deacons, and missionaries saying, "Wait a minute, brother, living from paycheck to paycheck is in no way comparable to living from faith to faith." Well, let us examine the context of my statement and just be open-minded for one minute. For many, "Living from paycheck to paycheck" has a negative connotation suggesting that we don't make enough, we may not be in the right job, or we just can't manage the little bit we make. Okay, now let us put some faith lens on that statement. To live from faith to faith literally means no matter how much you make or do not make your trust is not in the resource (money), but in the source (God); therefore, we trust the process by allowing Him to provide fresh manna to sustain us through any storm or battle we may encounter. Conversely, we do not rush the process by panicking even though we may not have everything we need at a given time or season.

This manna happens with **Serenity**, bringing peace in an ever-troublesome world; possibly the most often overlooked need in life. Psychologists suggest that there is no greater wealth than peace of mind. In essence, peace of mind is a state of being mentally and spiritually in harmony with your emotions daily. All too often, we seek things, gimmicks, and people to bring us comfort and peace, not knowing that there is one who is known as the "Prince of Peace" (Isaiah 9:6). He also assures us that "He would keep us in perfect peace whose mind is stayed on him" (Isaiah 26:3).

Finally, **Security** is the state of being free from danger or threats. This may seem the most impossible due to the threat of danger we face each day. Security may range from something as simple as home security, to the security of our nation against terrorist attacks, and domestic attacks, similar to those that took place on the U. S. Capitol on January 6, 2021, Inauguration Day! At the end of the day, there is no security like the security of being in and under the "Shadow of the Almighty" (Psalms 91:1)

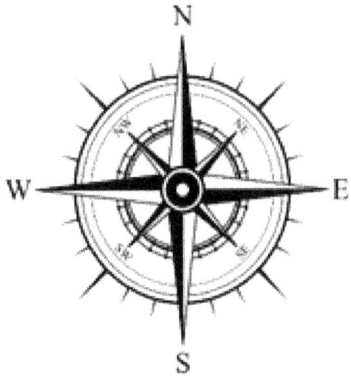

Chapter 3

The Basics

With each day that passes, we all continue to write and highlight our stories. Basic actions, interactions and conversations are how we should write our stories not through social media or other platforms. Never gauge your impact or influence on something/someone based on what others choose to do or not do, because it is not about them. It is about your purpose, process, and how you navigate through life. While these are life's basic tenets, we often overlook them because they do not always jump out at us.

Unpacking your Purpose

Our purpose is fundamental because it not only lauds the groundwork for who we are but also starts the building process of where we want to go. When our purpose (the why) settles, we can transition into other chapters and seasons of our life. The late Dr. Myles Munroe said it best *"When purpose is not known, abuse is inevitable."* Simply meaning, when you do not know the basics in life or your "why," abuse or "abnormal use" can become the norm. Many of us can attest to this when we go through that period or season when we try just about everything, hoping to fill that void, which happens when we secure our purpose. Our "why" is so critical because we can spend years chasing yesterday, not knowing that our today is the answer. I can recall when I was about 12 or 13 and met my first Basketball Coach in middle school. He was tough on us about winning, but he never taught us the fundamentals or basics. That included dribbling, shooting, rebounding, et cetera. He assumed that we knew these skills because we came out for tryouts. Fortunately, for me, I knew some of the basics, and I made the team. However, the tragedy with this situation, and so many more in life, is that only a few know the basics and never get the help necessary to be successful in making the team of life. Amazingly, when I moved to high school, I found a coach who taught me, coached me, and now is my longtime friend and mentor. He prepared me for the game of basketball and the game of life. Understanding your purpose and "your why" can take you places and open doors to your next chapter in life! Sometimes purpose puts life in perspective, and one's perspective can be everything at the end of the day. It is the recognition that you are not as great as people think when you hit the winning shot and not as bad as you feel when the same people crucify you for missing a similar shot! Moreover, we sometimes come to those pivotal moments when we must RESPOND (say something), REACT (do something) or RETALIATE (return something) to what someone said to us or about us; We must remember it's not always what you say, but many times it's in what you don't say that speaks volumes; at the end of the day, their ignorance doesn't minimize your intelligence just because they decided to put it on display! Know your purpose and stay true to it!

While purpose is basic for many of us, our passion is the fuel that keeps our purpose "lit."

Unpacking your Passion

Passion is essential to our purpose because it involves our emotions and feelings about something. Some days we may wear our feelings on our shoulders because of what someone said, and it is not always the best look. However, in light of everything we may face each day we can be confident God's love will see us through. Footnote, we must remember it is a thin line between confidence and arrogance. Confidence is when you know who you are and do not have to prove it to anybody. Arrogance is when you do not know who you are and trying to prove it to everybody. Therefore, with that said, we all may lose our fire or passion in life because of a setback or tragedy with someone we love. Although some bounce back in record time, others never recover. Thus, their purpose and passion are paralyzing in the process. These are the realities of when one loses the fire to move forward. One of the keys to recapturing the fire and our focus is to understand we may grow weary as time passes; however, the promises of God never grow old. Therefore, to build momentum to recapture our passion, we must not allow yesterday's obstacles to rob us of today's opportunities. With that said, I try to do three things every day, LISTEN more often than I talk, LEARN to appreciate the simple things in life, and LAUGH every day. I discovered that some things are just not that serious.

So often, we think overcoming trauma and tragedy is a one-time or overnight sensation. However, few accomplish many things overnight, but over time. That is why process is the next step to purpose and passion.

Unpacking the Process

Process involves a systematic series of ongoing actions with a desired end. Simply put, taking the necessary time to overcome your struggles without giving up. Another translation is "trusting the process and not rushing the process."

It is amazing what happens when we take the high road as we navigate the process. Consider what can happen in a moment; when faced with hater-raids, road rage, or blockades, we can go HIGH (trust the process, what goes around will eventually come around). We can go LOW (become who you are, not trying to prove who you are). Finally, we can go IN (releasing what you are not, wishing you could get it back).

Life is an amazing journey that is virtually impossible to go through without an injury or hurt by someone saying or doing something to you. Three ways to handle the situation; we can be BIGGER (recognizing that some things are not worth the time or effort to deal with). We can be BETTER (realizing that we learn some of our best lessons from the worst situations), or BITTER (resolving to live life mad at the world). It is like drinking poison and expecting everyone else to die. One of the keys to getting through these various processes in life is our perspective or way of thinking.

Perspective is one of the silent game changers in our life. Consider this, why do some people always seem to have it together even though we know they do not always have it together? It has a lot to do with perspective. ATTITUDE (how we handle things despite outside influences), APPROACH (our view/vision on situations that seem impossible), and APTITUDE (our ability to always see what "could be" and never what "can't be").

One of the most challenging feats of the process is that it takes us out of our comfort zone, particularly when it comes to growth. The amazing thing about growth is that it comes as a package deal that is usually uncomfortable. It's packed with PAIN (the equalizer for success), PROCESS (the bridge to meaningful promotion), and PROMISE (the results of waiting till it's your time)

After this journey, we are now ready for the transition or "next" move.

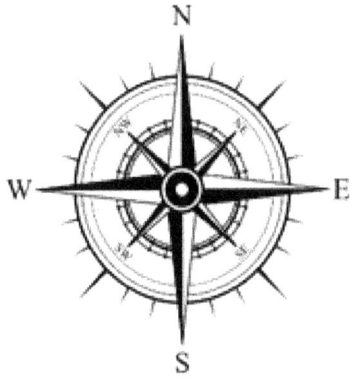

Chapter 4

The Transition

One of the most challenging assignments in life is transition, in non-technical language, making changes. It is more about MOVING from one thing to another (meaning you cannot stay where you are), MANAGING that movement (meaning that you must allow yourself the time to grow) and MONITORING your progress (meaning that you allow others to check you even when it hurts). Have you ever wondered why some days you are in the dump, and then other days you could conquer the world? It may be directly related to your connections, who, what, and where. There are three major connections in life; TRANSITIONAL people, those who develop you as you pass through different phases of life. TRANSACTIONAL people, those who drain you because it is always about what they can get from you and never to you. Finally, TRANSFORMATIONAL people check, challenge, and ultimately change you because of their connection to where you are going in life, not just, where you have been.

Unpacking Turning Points

Sometimes in life, we all reach those turning points, a time and season where a decisive change has to occur...when it does happen, we must be aware of those PITFALLS, hidden dangers waiting to put us in a snag. In addition, we must be mindful of POTHOLES, those places where we are stuck because we lose focus. Finally, the PUDDLES, the little water or things that can cause you to hydroplane out of control. It is never easy to admit when we end up in a puddle and cannot escape. I can recall when I was transitioning from State Government to working with the School System. When I started to teach, I did not intend to work full-time because I had semi-retired after almost 20 years as a Research Analyst/ Hearing Officer. I did not realize that I would be stuck in the "puddle" of teaching while I thought retirement was inevitable. Fast forward, I am now a Principal, and the transition has been nothing short of amazing. What I thought was a puddle, was the springboard or transition into my "next" chapter in life. Although some chapters and seasons may not be a part of the plan, the beauty is when we step out in faith and confidence, and the rewards are far above what we could ever imagine.

Unpacking Lasting Points

As we continue to turn the corner during transitional moments there will always be those lasting moments that leave an indelible mark on us. Although we may transition more than once, it is okay to hit the Refresh button; especially, since we all are stuck occasionally. Even though my transition from State Government to Local Government was a breath of fresh air, there are times that I still am stuck. The beginning of anything new is always fresh, but in some cases, our beginning does not necessarily determine the ending. During the transition, we must always REFLECT on where we have been. We must also INSPECT where we are now. Finally, what determines our future success is how well we PROJECT where we are going. Being open and honest with ourselves, regardless of where we are, always helps during all of our transitional moments.

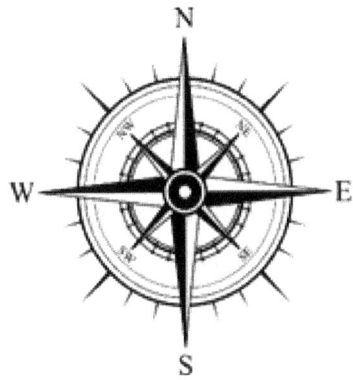

Chapter 5

The Transaction

Sometimes in our lives, we have felt like a transaction or a business deal. Especially when some people only call us when they need us. As bad as this may sound, we must accept part of the blame because we allow people to do it. One of the nuggets to navigating to our "next" is understanding the importance of closing one chapter while moving to another. In other words, not closing certain "apps" can cause you to spend unnecessary time on something that is over, but you do not know it.

Unpacking the deception

"Transactional relationships are built on expectations for reciprocation." Meaning everyone wants something in return, not necessarily something for nothing. It is strictly business. Both individuals are concerned and self-serving, ensuring they get as much as possible from the relationship.

While transitional people help us through life, we must be careful in dealing with transactional people. They drain you because it is always about what they can get from you and never to you. The major challenge with these individuals is that we can get snake bitten and not even realize it. In addition, when we are so eager to move into our new season, we must beware of the snakes that come out early to poison our purpose and detour our destiny. They come in all shapes and forms. Be aware of the water moccasins; they HANG around water to inject you with hatred. Watch out for the copperheads; they HIDE under rocks to inject you with hurt. Be watchful of the rattlesnakes; they HISS or inject you with a lot of noise but usually not saying anything. These are just the warning signs that come with new opportunities.

In addition, we must beware of "Window Shoppers." They can tell you everything from what you should, could, or would do, but in the end, they "won't do." They only see things from one perspective, the outside looking in. Consider coming inside for a change. In doing so, we will discover that our OBSERVATIONS, OPINIONS, and OUTLOOKS will change. It is amazing how differently we see things from the other side of the window.

Unpacking the real deal

While we can never avoid these individuals or situations, balance is the key to recognizing transactional people. However, the real deal is never being afraid to confront those transactional moments or conversations. Initially, it may feel uncomfortable, but in the end, it benefits you and everyone involved. I recall a situation with a friend of mine where he wanted to borrow some money and said he would pay it back on a specific day. My challenge was that the friend never paid back anything on time. Therefore, I had to decide whether to give the individual the money, not expect it back, or not give the individual the money at all. Here is the difference, if I gave him the money, there was no expectation for the return, but if I lent it and he did not return it as expected, I would be upset. As a side note, I knew this friend was "transactional" at best, but I still had to decide. I gave him the money (although I did not tell him that ☺), and he never returned it as promised. The beauty for me was I recognized that this individual was always taking but never giving. Sometimes we must come to grips with certain truths if we want to move to our "next." It may not be pleasant, and hurt for a moment, but the joy is in knowing this too shall pass, but I had to let them go for it to pass. If we want to move on from some people, we have to be willing to let them go. The real deal is that we do not lose anything in the process when it is simply a transaction. We actually gain peace of mind!

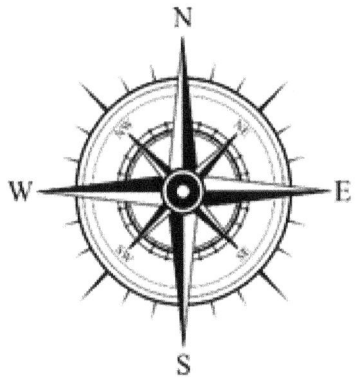

Chapter 6

The Transformation

Transformation is one of the hardest things in life because in nonprofessional terms, it is all about change. Most, if not all of us, struggle with change because we are creatures of habit. We do the same things every day, go the same way every day, and spend time with the same people every day, so I would guess we don't necessarily like change. However, moving into your "next season" or chapter must be about change: how you respond and adjust. It is never easy or comfortable, but learning to adjust early helps you through the process. The beauty is that some people change with time others change when you learn to let them go, so they can eventually grow.

In addition, TRANSFORMATIONAL people check, challenge, and ultimately change you because of their connection to where you are going in life, not just, where you have been in life. When I switched from being a research analyst to a teacher, it was frustrating because I was more involved with data in research, but in teaching, it was the people or students behind the data. The irony, however, is that after teaching the students, I eventually had to return to the data. Any good teacher knows that data drives instruction. In other words, staying on top of instructional trends and the latest data regarding those trends keeps you on the cutting edge as an educator!

Although transformative thinking can set you apart, it is not always easy when you suffer a setback after taking risks to make a difference. One of the most difficult things is learning how to "Bounce Back." This Challenges most of us because it seems like the end of the world at that moment, and nothing else matters. However, the key to getting through is to remember NOTHING comes to stay... it eventually will pass...It may SHAKE us...SHOCK us...or even SHATTER our dreams for the moment...but we will "Bounce Back."

Unpacking the Shock

For many of us, we all have been through seasons where the shock of something almost took us out. I can recall when my daughter got pregnant; I was the last to find out.

Although the initial shock had me, reeling because I knew this would change my daughter's life forever. I did not realize that it would bring me more joy than I could ever imagine as a grandfather. Some things may look bad for the moment, but they can be good when we see them through a different set of lenses. Additionally, some things that may shock us during one phase of life are the things that shape us for our next season. After 12 years, my grandson spends more time with me every summer and has added a few years to my life. Moreover, I do so much with him and for him throughout the year; it is almost as if he is my son. As time passes, life packages things differently as we move to our next chapter in life. What is familiar to us now may look different, as we remain open to change. Never miss the opportunity to explore your "next" simply because it is "packaged" with what we may perceive as a mistake or a bad decision. Some decisions, as bad as they may seem, could be the one that changes the course of an entire nation, let alone a family. The challenge for us as we continue to navigate to our "next" is to remain open, honest, and sensitive to the seasonal shifts that come with change!

Unpacking the Shame

Sometimes the hardest thing to overcome when we decide to move on is shame. While it was difficult as a pastor and leader in a small community to embrace the idea that my daughter was pregnant, if I would ever move to my "next,"

I had to embrace it. As tough as it was for me, I am sure it was tougher on my daughter because she never wanted to bring any shame on me as a pastor. However, I soon realized that it was not about me at all. It was about supporting my daughter. She was moving into a chapter of her life that would change everything, and I knew she needed me. At that point, I told her that Pastoring is what I do, but being a father is who I am. From that point on, a transformation took place in our relationship. I might add the church was just as supportive. This experience was such a learning experience for my family and me. We spend so much time trying to protect, preserve and prevent certain things from happening, but the truth is that life happens to all of us. It is not what happens that shifts the paradigm but how we respond. My daughter and grandson are doing well. I might add another pastor friend of mine experienced a similar situation and reached out to me for guidance. I was glad to be able to share with him how the "Grace of God" guided me through the process!

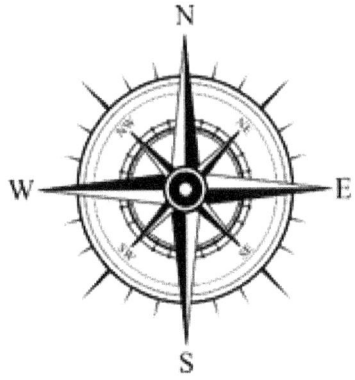

Chapter 7

The Failure

Sometimes we all fail miserably in life, and we wonder if we will ever get a chance to do things over again. While many may subscribe to the notion that "first impressions are lasting impressions," I also believe that first impressions do not have to be final impressions if we know how to bounce back from the setback. With each day that passes and the amount of bad news that travels around the world at warp speed, it is a wonder that good news can ever get a word in edgewise. Nevertheless, let me remind you, "As cold water is to a thirsty soul, so is good news from a far country." However, knowing the SOURCE is the key to finding, following, and focusing on the good news. (Not the one bringing or carrying a bone, but the one who can stop the bone) Knowing when to remain SILENT. (Especially when that same news that goes around will eventually come back around, and those who we expose now may be the ones who have to defend us later) Finally, knowing where to SHOUT, from the rooftop to the valley, from the hood to the woods, some news can't be denied. When you look back from where He bought you to where no one could take you, that's good news!

As things begin to slow down, one of the most challenging assignments in life is moving forward while trying to let go. Perhaps this is one of life's tallest orders because some setbacks leave such a damaging scar that we lose the will to engage again.

Unpacking Scars that Remind Us But Do Not Define Us

During my first year in college, I was a part of the basketball team, which was a great feeling. However, to stay on the team, we had to keep our grades up. Unfortunately, I had some challenges with my US History class and did not pass it my first year. It was not only a wake-up call, but I almost lost my scholarship because of my failure. What bothered me throughout the entire process was that I thought I was fine in the class because I played basketball, and the professor would ask each day how we were doing. However, failing the class helped me understand that nothing is given but earned. I thought just because the professor was cordial with me every day, he would "give me a grade" since I was on the team. What is so amazing about this story is that after 40-plus years, it still reminds me but does not define me.

Moreover, I never expected anything else from anybody after that semester unless I earned it. It made me a better person, player, and now principal. What could have scarred me for the rest of my life only redefined my priorities, purpose, and plans for my "next" season. I could have been upset with the professor because I felt "played," but ultimately, we are responsible for our actions and assumptions. The fact that I failed to study, as I should have to pass the class, only served as a reminder that no matter how cordial a person is, it does not excuse us from doing the work we are assigned. Assuming that being a basketball player gave me a sense of entitlement made matters worse.

Unpacking the Scars to be a Better Person

Because of the scars, I am a better person. The following semester, I took the time to find a tutor to help me with my history class, and consequently, I passed. Although I passed with a "C," I was excited because I earned the grade. Sometimes, when people give us favors, props, and free passes, we never feel the satisfaction of achieving something on our merits. In this case, I earned the grade, and the teacher that tutored me through this process became a mentor throughout my time in college.

Interestingly, other players became a part of my study group after I shared with them what happened to me. Becoming a better person also included making wiser decisions for the remainder of my college tenure. This does not mean I made all the right decisions. However, in my decisions, I always took into account that my actions would speak louder than my words. For example, if I told someone I would be at a specific place to do something, I tried to keep my word and not make excuses. Sometimes our excuses speak louder than our actions. Excuses are "tools of incompetence that build monuments of nothing, and those who specialize in them will seldom accomplish anything. Thus, I tried to keep my word, good or bad. This is not always easy because, many times, we want to please everybody. However, sometimes we have to learn to say no. Saying no does not always mean we do not want to but just not now. That was one of my challenges then and now because we hate to let people down. Since that time, it is not about letting people down but me staying afloat. My social and emotional well-being is much more important than worrying about the feeling of others just because I said no!

Unpacking the Scars to Find Your Purpose

Sometimes, when we do not know our "Why," we experience pain without purpose; for example, so many of us spend years in a profession because it is a job and not a career, or it is what we have to do, not what we want to do. Consequently, we hate waking up every morning, going to the same job every day, and dealing with the same people every week. While this may seem brutal, the sad thing is that we continue to do it year after year. The fear of what others think or say keeps us from risking doing or trying something different. As I have often shared, "If we allow fear to change who we are, it will change where we are going. "One of the most pivotal decisions in my life was when I left state government as a hearings officer to go into teaching. Teaching is a part of my purpose and reason for being born. However, it was not until I decided to do something about it that things changed for me. As a result, what I thought was a setback when laid off due to a reduction in force was one of the life-changing comebacks of my life. I became a career switcher, from adjudicator to educator. As I moved into a different chapter, I never imagined that this chapter would bring me to my destiny and ultimate purpose. Sometimes what looks like a setback is just a setup for a major comeback. This was major for me because now I am a principal not only affecting lives but also helping young people find their purpose and flourish in the process.

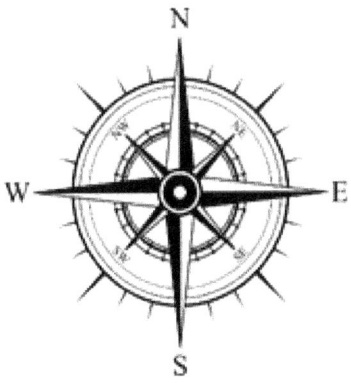

Chapter 8

The Faith

As we continue to navigate the new seasons and chapters after the various setbacks, the one thing necessary in moving forward is faith, the ability to believe in yourself when nobody else believes in you. This is necessary because we often find ourselves in crisis mode due to local, social, or global issues. When this happens, we can see three narratives emerging during these times. First are the DEFINING moments. Those moments are when we recognize who the true source is and stop depending on a resource. No matter what the person brings to the table. Secondly, there are REMINDING moments. Those moments we realize if the Lord brought us out before, he could certainly do it again, even though the promise may take longer than the process. Finally, there are those BLINDING moments. Those moments are when we rationalize with the "why" things happen instead of focusing on the "who" can make it happen. At the end of the day, if God can create man and the world in 6 days, certainly He can turn our situation around in a matter of moments!

Unpacking the Fear that Blocks our Faith

While many factors may affect, influence, and challenge our faith, the one factor that changes the game for many of us is fear. Fear is a faith blocker. It blocks our ability to believe the impossible because of the noise of others in the background. The fear of what others SAY (Short-term memory). The fear of what others SEE (Impaired Vision). The fear of our success (Self-inflicted wounds). Fear is no more than a passenger we allow to ride with us daily. However, if we allow it to change who we are, it will change where we go! This is why it is so important that we watch who we allow to ride with us and what people say to us. Their words could be faith blockers. Words are the fuel that, in many cases, propel our FAITH...perpetuate our FEAR...or pull us into FOOLISHNESS. However, here is the game changer, whose pumping your fuel? Sometimes, we get it twisted; the fuel does make a difference. The difference between who you are, what you are, and where you are. It is all about self-service, full service, or no service.

Consider Faith (STARTS) our engine again when life becomes a buildup of corrosion; Faith (STABILIZES) our engine when we lose confidence in those who we thought were our substance, but soon realize they should never have been. Finally, Faith (STAMPS) us, letting us know that we can go anywhere in the world with the proper postage.

Unpacking the Fight For Our Faith

While there are many fights that we all encounter in life, the most engaging is the fight for our faith. It gets hard at times, but we must continue The Fight despite the foolishness that comes at times unexpectedly. We must still hold on to our FAITH. Despite our failures, we must maintain our grip on our faith. Finally, focusing on our faith is the one thing that pushes us to the end and causes us to finish strong. The beauty of faith is that it is in our DNA.

Another thing that we must remember about the fight for our faith is that it is a thin line between confidence and arrogance. Faith is the confidence that you know who you are and do not have to prove it to anybody. On the other hand, arrogance is you do not know who you are and try to prove it to everybody. Our assignment is to know the difference, walk in it, live by it, and demonstrate it daily. Although we might struggle to demonstrate our faith daily, knowing that we are in the battle makes all the difference. I can recall one of my greatest battles with faith when I was in the last chapter of my dissertation. I had completed all the research and was waiting for final approval. Waiting is almost a battle within itself, especially when patience is not one of your strongest attributes. One week felt like one year, but I finally got the approval, and my dissertation was complete. In life, we cannot rush the process, but we have to trust the process.

Unpacking the Multiple Lens of Faith

Another aspect of faith is seeing through multiple sets of lenses. For example, some of us see faith through one of three sets of lenses: nearsighted, farsighted, or no lens at all. Nearsighted lens are those lenses where we only see people where they are but not where they can be in the future. Farsighted lens is where we only see people at a distance but never see what they can do working closely with us. This is critical because we need to invest in people to know what they can bring to the table and us personally. Finally, when we have no vision at all, we always are critical of any and everybody because we cannot see. One of my greatest life lessons as a leader was learning to see people through multiple lens sets. For example, as a young leader, I realized I was eager and zealous about people coming to the church and trusted everybody for face value. However, as time progressed, I realized I had a shortsighted vision; my heart led my decisions instead of my head. This can be detrimental to ministry and relationships, especially when trying to bounce back from a setback. In addition, when you are hurt in the process, trust becomes a factor that can hinder you from moving on to your next chapter in life. Fortunately, for me, as I got older and wiser, I allowed my heart to guide me while my head would anchor me in my decision-making process. Although my lens was refined in the process, I also discovered, as I got older, that it is okay to use a zoom lens when your nearsightedness may be a struggle. It is seeing people where they are and where they can be.

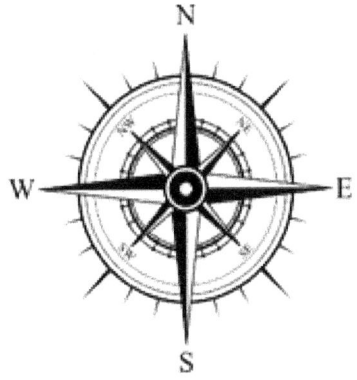

Chapter 9

The Follow-Up

The one thing that is a game changer for so many is follow-up or the lack thereof. I remember my first opportunity to get a real job after graduating from college. I failed to follow up and follow through. I interviewed well for the job as a research analyst and had to follow up with the manager the next day by phone. Unfortunately, I got busy the next day with my friends and failed to call the manager back. As it turned out, I called the day after, and someone else got the job. Although I got another job later that month, I was disappointed. Sometimes just calling someone back, sending an email, or acknowledging can make all the difference in the world. Some systems are set to prevent us from making the most out of bad situations. In addition, with everything happening locally, socially, and even globally, the challenge for many of us is not moving so fast through life. In doing so, we do not get the chance to genuinely TASTE... TOUCH... and TELL... our story. Hint: Slow down for a moment, and we can appreciate ALL of the ingredients in life and not just some of them!

One of my favorite movies that I perhaps have watched over ten times is "Top Gun Maverick." The movie keeps you on the edge of your seat, but one part really does it for me. After an intense argument with the instructor regarding what it would take to fly a successful mission, "Rooster" whose father flew with Maverick before he died, tells the instructor, "It's not the plane but the pilot who makes the difference in the mission." This statement is classic. So often in life we think it is the "system" that is holding us back, but in actuality, it is the person. Some systems in life appear stacked against us. For example, someone rarely comes out of high school or off the street to get a corporate job or employment in the front office. However, the system teaches us that it is not what you know but whom you know. This may be true, but the system cannot stop you from putting the time in and pushing the envelope until you get to a place where you can make a difference. Although systems may be a set of things, working together as parts of a larger network or interconnecting system, we still make a difference. As it turned out, in the movie 'Top Gun Maverick," it was the pilot that made the difference in shooting down the enemy with an underachieving F-14 plane. Sometimes the system may force us to use equipment and material that may seem antiquated. However, it is not the system but the ones who can navigate around and through the system.

Unpacking the Growing Pains

Unpacking growing pains is sometimes painful when we're accustomed to people using the "system" as an excuse for hard work or a pass to blame someone for their lack of effort. Growing pains are always hard to deal with primarily because if we ever want to be successful in anything, we must continue to grow. Nothing stops despite the setbacks, seasonal shifts, and systemic changes in life. In fact, the minute we stop growing, we start the death process. We call this process rigor mortis; when this happens, one becomes hard, hateful, and hell to deal with. Sometimes our next chapter or season may take a minute, but we must learn to trust the process and not rush the process. What we may think happens overnight actually happens over time. One of the most challenging lessons I learned as a coach, pastor, and principal, those individuals who look like they got it all together really do not have it together. It takes a wise leader to discern situations like this because we all want to look the part even if we do not feel the part.

However, the truth is that looks are deceiving, and those who can recognize this will usually be the ones who can help you in the end. Growing pains are necessary if we will move into our next season. Remember, it is not always, how we react to the pain but how we manage it.

Unpacking the Changes, We Cannot Control

As we get older, we must all remember that change is the only constant thing, even if we cannot control it. While I wear many hats daily, one of the most challenging is that of a principal. The challenges are great because every day is different. The moment I try to set something in stone as it relates to improving the culture and climate of the school, a student does something, or an event happens that changes my perspective.

Some things I can control by putting corrective measures in place, and then there are times when the corrective measures only create another issue. In essence, to be successful as an instructional leader, it's not just about the data that drives the instruction but understanding the culture and climate of the school. Then, being willing to change if necessary and admitting what you thought would work did not work. Change is not just about the climate and culture; it is often about us as individuals, willing to change how we do things and see things. I have always stood back for years and waited to see what would happen. Especially as one who has always seen through the lens of "old school" administration, do it because I told you, not necessarily, because it works. However, over the years, I have found that modeling what you want to see and getting involved with the students at "pep rallies" and other school-wide events make a significant difference. *"Change becomes a reality when we become the change; we want to see in others."* (Gandhi)

Unpacking How to Move In Silence

Sometimes following up does not require any talk but action. Many of us err when we think we must make a public announcement instead of responding silently. To follow up means to take action. Now in some cases, we have to respond verbally, but in most cases, our actions will speak much louder than our words. One of the most frustrating things about someone not following up is that most think it is a small matter. The worse feeling is when you ask someone why they did not call you back, and they respond, "Oh, I did not think it was that important." If it was important for them to leave a message and to take the time to call, then maybe it is important to call back. There are many reasons why some choose not to follow up or respond. However, answering in silence can speak volumes. I recall an incident at school with a student who had become embarrassed by a situation. When I got all the facts, many wanted me to make an announcement on the intercom, calling out everybody involved. After careful consideration, I emailed all the parties and talked with the parents, and everybody was pleased. Sometimes we may think that grandstanding or trying to make someone feel the way others feels is the answer. By moving in silence and not publicizing the situation, everybody was pleased. Most of us want to know that someone hears us without everybody talking about us. It is never easy to follow up with a sensitive issue and move in silence to protect all parties.

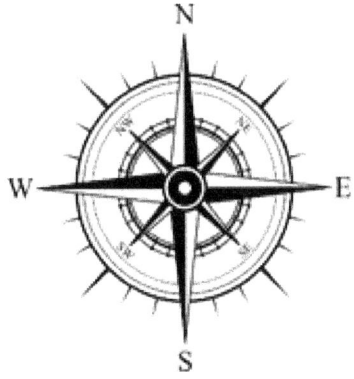

Chapter 10

The Call

Life is a composite of many calls; however, the call that often makes the difference is one we respond to and follow through. Throughout my life, my calls have been to preach, pastor, be a principal, mentor, community leader, and so on. The one call that has been the most rewarding is the call to make a difference. What I have discovered as time passed, it is not the vocation, field, or assignment but our response to the call. So many of us wait for a "clarion call" for a particular assignment or vocation, but that may never come. However, our response is the one thing that determines our success and fulfillment in the call. Just the acceptance can sometimes position us for the "unexpected blessings" that can spill over to other chapters in our life. I can recall when I had just completed college and was looking for a good job. My mother was a custodian, and she was good at her job. She often told me it is not the job that makes us great but the person behind it. She was also good at building relationships wherever she worked. One of the facilities she cleaned was a state building, which happened to be the unemployment office. She asked if I would be willing to work temporarily if she could talk with the manager to get me the job. Of course, I told her yes. I got the job. Although it was a temporary job, I knew if I did well, it could become permanent.

After about 3-4 months, a permanent position became available, and I was hired. Amazingly, responding to one call changed my life and opened the door to many other calls. I started as a research analyst, later a senior analyst, and eventually a hearings officer. As a side note, I worked for that same State Office for an additional 15 years. Sometimes the call is a bridge to a greater season and chapter later in life. As a young college graduate, I never thought my mother, an excellent custodian, would open the door for me to become a leader in the community 40 years later. Although my mother is no longer here to celebrate many of my accomplishments, the fact that she planted the seed and allowed me to grow speaks to her legacy, which will never die as I continue to grow.

Unpacking the Pitfalls Behind The Call

Although some calls may lead us into our next successful chapter in life, some are more challenging to navigate. As a young budding leader, not even at the ripe old age of 16, I felt called to the ministry of preaching. My grandmother, who had a tremendous influence on my life, and her being a minister almost felt like my destiny. At an early age, the challenge of this call was that I still had "some wild oats still to sow." However, my grandmother kept me so close to her that I did not get to sow "wild oats" or any oats. Sometimes we focus on the "glitz and glamor" of the call but do not realize the responsibility that comes with it. The pitfall for me was navigating high school as an athlete but remaining faithful to the call. There were days when I felt I was on top of the world and others when I thought I had let everybody down. However, what got me through the tough days was remaining true to who I was, not who I was trying to become. Sometimes we forget that "to become" is not overnight but over time. As time passed, I learned to navigate from ministry to athlete. There were also days when the expectation for me was to be an "overnight sensation," but forgetting it was a "lifetime journey." Now that it has been 40 years since the call, I have learned the art of managing the pitfalls and pain that come with the call.

Unpacking the Detours Behind The Call

Over the last few years, life has been anything but normal, especially for those who experienced health issues because of the pandemic and those who ultimately loss their lives or loved ones during the pandemic. In addition, some experienced detours toward their destiny and temporary setbacks before their ultimate comeback. Even with the detours and the setbacks, it only served as a springboard and pushed many of us into our next season and chapter. However, the relevant question for some is how to navigate the detours and setbacks when we have never been this way. Moreover, how do you bounce back from what appears to be a fatal setback? One of the first steps to navigating the setbacks is recognizing that not all are fatal, even though they may seem at the time. In the movie, "Top Gun Maverick," after over 30 years of service as one of the Navy's top aviators, Pete "Maverick" Mitchell is where he belongs. He constantly pushes the envelope as a courageous test pilot, dodging the rank advancement that would ground him. Training a detachment of graduates for a special assignment, Maverick must confront the ghosts of his past and his deepest fears, culminating in a mission that demands the ultimate sacrifice from those who choose to fly it. There is a clip in the movie where Maverick blew it royally when two of the pilots, he was training went down doing a maneuver and almost died. As a result, Maverick's job as the instructor was over. In addition, the admiral, who was not too fond of Maverick, replaced him and changed the entire routine.

Maverick was very disappointed, crushed, and felt it was over for him. However, a dear friend counseled Maverick and told him not to give up and that he would find a way to make it happen. He ended up not only getting his pilots back, but he also became the leader of the squadron he trained, and they were successful in their mission. The lesson, proper counsel, and following instructions can lead to a comeback from a potentially fatal setback. Often when we experience failure, we must guard our "ear gates" because too many folks in your ears make things unclear! Always have a trusted friend who will tell you what you need to hear and not always what you want to hear.

Unpacking the Pain Behind The Call

While there are pitfalls and detours behind the call, there is nothing like the pain behind the call. Sometimes we get excited about various assignments and positions, but we never know the emotional and psychological pain that comes with the call. To put this in perspective, I must refer to another movie, "The Equalizer," starring Denzel Washington. In summary, Robert McCall (Denzel Washington), a man of mysterious origin who believes he has put the past behind him, dedicates himself to creating a quiet new life. However, he cannot walk away when he meets Teri (Chloë Grace Moretz), a teenager manhandled by violent Russian mobsters. With his formidable skills, McCall emerges from self-imposed retirement and appears as an avenging angel, ready to take down anyone who brutalizes the helpless. Many of us in the ministry, particularly pastors, sometimes feel like guardian angels and cannot walk away from trying to help everybody.

The pain comes when you help those who later turn on you. It is not just that they turn on you but treat you as if they never knew you. Much like the "equalizer," you drop everything to help them, but somehow, they forget. Even though the pain is a part of the process, some pain never disappears, especially from those we invested so much. Sometimes things happen, and we all have experienced hurt, or others felt we had hurt them. However, there is no pain like when others hurt you. The key to moving forward, regardless of what side of the pain we are on, is to stop REHEARSING IT (playing it over again), stop NURSING IT (feeding and allowing it to grow again) but DISPERSE IT (let it go) to the one who can ultimately REVERSE IT (and make you whole again). I call this the ultimate pain reliever.

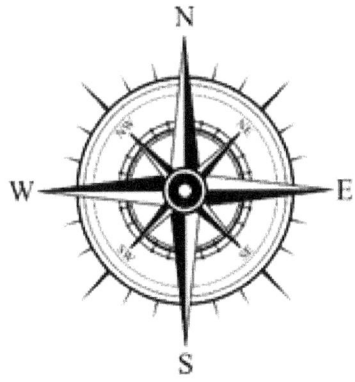

Chapter 11

The Commitment

One of the most challenging things about commitment is when you make up your mind to change, and you cannot because you are committed to a system, a particular way of doing things but do not know how to move away from that system. Commitment is the state or quality of dedication to a cause, activity, or something. This is much like growing up in a traditional church, always doing things a certain way, but when you got older; you wanted to do things differently. However, when you are stuck in a system, you have been committed to all your life, which is all you know. While certain systems may promote the negative side of commitment, there are also some positives.

I always remind others and myself about the story of the chicken, cow, and pig regarding the importance of committing to something and not just contributing. This is critically important when moving into our next season or chapter in life. Often some mean well, and they try to suggest that we contribute to our success instead of committing. In the story of the chicken, cow, and pig, they all came together due to a catastrophic event on the farm with the other animals. They all agreed to bring something to the table for breakfast to ease the pain of what had happened. The chicken agreed to bring the eggs to the breakfast since he was familiar with the situation. The cow agreed to bring the milk and indicated it would be no problem. The pig thought for a moment because they all suggested he bring the bacon to the breakfast. After careful consideration, the pig declared, I cannot bring the bacon because it requires a "total commitment" (death) for me, but it is only a contribution for the rest. Moving to the next chapter and phase of our life requires total commitment, body, soul, and spirit to succeed during the transition. There will be those around us, namely the "peanut gallery" suggestion that it does not require all of that, but we must remind them contributions will not do, only those willing to give their all.

Unpacking the Cost Behind Our Commitment

We all have heard the terminology, "You must pay the cost to be the boss." After hearing this some 40 years ago, this saying still holds true. Some want to lead and be out front but do not want to commit. Leading requires commitment, and commitment requires time. Going back to my favorite movie, "Top Gun Maverick," at the beginning of the movie, Maverick faced the decision of flying one of their newest planes to reach a certain speed or the entire program folding because the admiral felt that there was no more money in the budget for the program. Because he was committed to the men he led, Maverick took the risk of losing his job to save the jobs of those he managed. Because the benefits outweighed the risk, he flew the plane. Although Maverick reached the speed to keep the program afloat, he still faced losing his command as the captain. Upon his return, his crew was elated that he made the speed, but he lost his command of that crew. Although he lost his command, one of his old friends, who happened to be an admiral, reassigned him to another command as an instructor. The beauty of this story is that when committed to more than just what benefits you, things will ultimately work out. As it turns out, his new assignment was perhaps one of his greatest contributions as a Navy aviator. The cost or risk he took for his crew propelled him to his "next chapter" as a pilot and instructor. We may never know our ultimate destiny in life; however, the willingness to take risks and make certain commitments always works in our favor.

Unpacking the Purpose Behind Our Commitment

The late Myles Munroe once stated, *"Where purpose is not known, abuse is inevitable."* When we do not know why something exists and the reason behind its creation, chances are we will abuse (abnormally use) it. Too often, we see and hear of child abuse, human trafficking, and other forms of mishandled children. This usually occurs because we lose sight of our "why." When it happens, we end up in places and spaces that do not serve us well. For example, when I finished my first book, "Menspiration," followed by the workbook, I later started on my next book but never could get beyond chapter three. I spent almost two or three years trying to sit down to write but could never get the urge to stay with it. Now that I am almost through chapter 11 of the book, I now understand the power behind our purpose. Rediscovering our "why" in everything we do simplifies life and other things. After an intense argument with a dear friend and them calling me out, I knew then the importance of my "why." All too often, we spend wasted years doing things just because it was convenient or we felt compelled to, but we never really seek our purpose in the process. In writing this book, after my dear friend shared with me, I rediscovered my why, and my writing flowed.

Of course, there were some days when my thoughts were all over the place, but it was not a struggle for the most part. Our commitment to the next assignment will follow when we understand our space and place in life. I hope that you will be excited as I am when you lock into your "why."

Unpacking Quality Relationships Behind Our Commitment

Relationship without commitment is akin to lungs with no air. As we develop relationships throughout our lives, there are those for a season, those for a reason, and those for a lifetime. Although our next chapter or season may sometimes appear to be frightening, the key to moving forward is to trust the process. The process is systemic and ongoing but has a desired end in mind. Even though the process may take time, it is essential to trust the process and not rush the process. After 30 years in ministry, 25 years in education, and 15 years serving on local boards, the one thing that I have learned is that things happen over time, but not overnight. In addition, I have done more in my life on the other side of 50 rather than on the front side. As the next chapter and season unfold, you must assess where you are, adjust to the new season, and then realign for your "next." Sometimes the relationships we may think were for a lifetime may have been for a season. However, the only way to determine if it was for a lifetime is to be willing to forge ahead to your next chapter. Although we will never know what tomorrow holds, knowing who holds tomorrow helps us through the process. It may appear scary, but as things unfold and you continue to trust the process, things will make sense. When I moved to Lawrenceville, Virginia, over 35 years ago to start the third phase of my career, I never thought this would be where the Lord would develop me to be the leader and public servant that changed my life. As I prepare for my "next," I am excited to see what relationships and commitments will unfold.

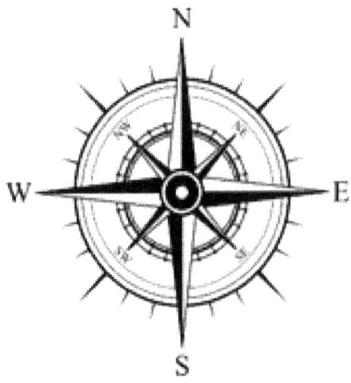

Chapter 12

The Commission

Every chapter in life comes with a mixture of joy along the journey and pain within the process; however, with any good book, one chapter ends while another begins. As we pivot from the seasons, setbacks, and systems towards the beginning of your "next," I am excited to commission you to rewrite your narrative. The undeniable possibilities, unmistakable potential, and unmatched promises are yours for the asking. Although, at times, it may be bitter and sweet, your next phase stands waiting for you to make that deciding move. There are times in life when we all get weary. We can have some of our worst encounters, even on the best of days. Yet the key to getting through our struggles is to remain FOCUSED on the prize and not the problem...keep the FAITH, release the fear..., and do not lose your FIRE because of foolishness. One of the most challenging things about the commissioning process is battling the growing pains. Growing pains are always hard to deal with primarily because if we ever want to be successful in anything, we must continue to grow. The minute we stop growing, we start the death process. When rigor mortis sets in, we become HARD... HATEFUL...and HELL to deal with. It is amazing that dead people cannot talk, dream, or impart vision. They no longer have a voice in anything. Therefore, we must make the most of our life and the opportunities that still await.

Unpacking the Next Season

So often, we fail to realize that there are four seasons in life. Each season has nuggets to help us navigate through them all. However, the key to moving forward is recognizing the nuggets in each season and paying attention to the climate and traffic signs. The climate will indicate the seasonal shifts, and the weather patterns usually will follow. Although there are four seasons, we can usually tell the difference by the change in temperature. The traffic signs are to alert you of what is ahead. Some signs may be obscure or hidden, but they are usually visible to indicate what to expect. With that said, you can recognize the shift and seasonal changes in your life when certain people and things start to fall off, and new relationships emerge. Perhaps you are in the "fall" or "autumn" of your life, and winter is getting ready to set in. We cannot be afraid to move into our season when this seasonal shift occurs. If we fail to do so, we miss our "next" season and risk staying in the "fall" of our lives. Even though winter may bring the "cold attitudes" and the "snowy conditions" that make it difficult to move into your season, it is also the preparation for spring and your growth. Recognizing and applying these simple analogies will make life much easier to navigate. Finally, as we move into the spring and summer of our lives, we must be aware that growth brings challenges. As the "green grass" grows and looks beautiful, we must remember to cut it when it gets too tall. As we grow into our next season, we must guard against leeches and insects attaching themselves to us. We must prepare to cut people off to continue the process of growing and maturing. Few of us like to cut the grass, but somebody must. Nothing is worse than a beautiful house, but the grass is so tall you cannot enjoy it. Remember to keep growing and staying on the cutting edge of your next season; pruning people, places, and processes are necessary.

Unpacking the Setbacks/Setups

One of the most challenging things about setbacks is to know when to stop chasing yesterday. The tragedy with chasing yesterday is that it paralyzes your potential for today and prolongs the possibilities for tomorrow. In any new season or opportunity, there will always be those jealous of you. The sad commentary is that they do not even know you or anything about you, just what they heard about you. Therefore, unfortunately, you must be aware of those who will try to set you up or get you to fall. Some setups may appear to be setbacks, but they prepare us for major comebacks. One of the classic examples is the Biblical account in the book of Esther. When Haman saw that Mordecai did not bow or pay him homage, he was outraged. This attitude is similar to those who become upset and jealous of you when you move into your "next," It appears you have changed your circle of friends and no longer need them or "bow to them." As a result, Haman plotted to kill all the Jews and get the king to sign off on it. He failed to realize that God was on the side of the Jews and what he meant for evil; God would turn it around for good. What people try to do to you and plot against you cannot overtake you when God is with you. Mordecai's success hinged upon his obedience to the Lord. There will be times when we know that people are plotting and planning for us to fail, but when God is for us, he is more than the whole world against us. Therefore, the initial Setback for Mordecai was the Setup for a major comeback. Haman did not know that Esther had gained favor with the king, and she would become the "Equalizer" to free the entire nation. She went to the king on behalf of her people, and her words still resonate today "If I perish, let me perish, but I'm going to see the King!" Sometimes God will use the most unlikely person to be a part of your deliverance and your major comeback. Instead of the Jews failing, Haman failed in his attempt to destroy them. The irony was that Haman was destroyed by what he thought would destroy the Jews.

Unpacking the Systems

As we close the book, we must put a few words on the systems to rest. First, dealing with systems has always been around. We hear the old saying, "The system is stacked against us," "You cannot beat the system, "or lastly, "The system never changes." While all these sayings may be true, allowing "any system" to stop us or serve as a roadblock to our success is nothing short of an excuse. Many of us already know that "excuses are tools of incompetence that build monuments of nothing, and those who specialize in them will seldom accomplish anything." In essence, excuses have never helped anyone. As we move to our "next," it is critically important we understand that no matter if it's an "organizational system," a system of government," or even a judicial system, we make a difference. We can never let those who do not know us write our story. As the late Dr. Martin Luther King once shared, "*The ultimate measure of a man is not where he stands in moments of comfort and convenience, but where he stands at times of challenge and controversy.*" Although certain systems, such as segregation or critical race theory, have created ongoing racial division among certain cultures and our educational system, we still cannot allow it to stop us from moving to our "next." As an educator, pastor, and community leader, it is when we know that "we stand on the shoulders of others" that we keep me going and continuing the fight.

Moreover, we have an inherent obligation to the next generation and those who stand on our heels to keep pushing the narrative that "we can do better" and we will do better! We must also remember some days; sometimes we all want to go there. However, do not stay there. At the end of the day, your VOICE is too valuable to lose over nonsense; your VALUE is too vital to jeopardize your worth; finally, your VALIDATION is not by a few who do not know you but by the one who created you!

Therefore, know your worth, and let us step together as we navigate life's seasons, setbacks, and systems!

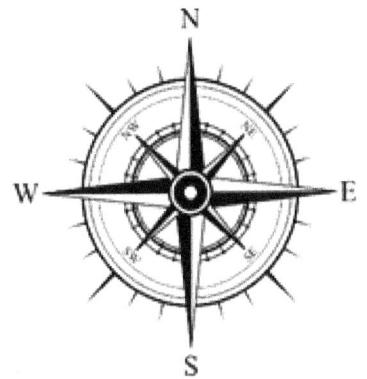

-NEXT-

ABOUT THE AUTHOR

Dr. Ronald Thornhill, a native of Richmond, VA, epitomizes a diverse persona—a devoted father, pastor, coach, educator, and author—each facet illuminated by his unwavering commitment to God and humanity. Revered as the "Community's Pastor," his resonant message of hope, healing, and spiritual liberation resonates across all levels of society, sparking a profound transformation throughout Southside, VA.

As the senior pastor of The Tabernacle of Zion Church in Lawrenceville, Virginia, Dr. Thornhill serves as a beacon of faith and inspiration, having founded this thriving ministry three decades ago. Beyond the pulpit, his influence extends as Principal at Brunswick High School, and as a board member for the MCV Community Memorial Hospital, the esteemed chair of the board for Southside Virginia Community College, and the Brunswick County Industrial Development Authority. Through his weekly podcast and social media posts, he consistently serves as a beacon of encouragement for numerous listeners, nurturing their souls with his blend of wisdom and compassion.

Dr. Thornhill's academic journey is illustrious, marked by achievements including a Bachelor's Degree in Business from Virginia Commonwealth University, a Master's Degree in Education from Old Dominion University, a Master's of Divinity from Virginia Union University, and a Doctorate Degree in Administration and Educational Leadership from Nova Southeastern University. Notably, he is also a proud member of Kappa Alpha Psi Fraternity, Incorporated.

Additionally, Dr. Thornhill is the author of the book and workbook entitled *Menspiration: Motivating & Inspiring Men to Conquer Life's Mountains

In addition to his professional pursuits, Dr. Thornhill finds solace and joy in his cherished family life. Alongside his wife, Patrice, who co-pastors with him, they are blessed with a daughter, Ashley, and a son, Ronald II. Their grandson, Joshua Josiah, adds an extra layer of delight, especially during their treasured summer moments together.

For speaking engagements, conferences, book signings, and to join the national book tour, please contact:

Email: thornhillronald1@gmail.com
X (formerly Twitter): @drthornhill23
Facebook: menspirations

MENSPIRATION MOMENT

Many have said it's not how you start but how you finish...but let's flip the script a little bit...how many of us have missed opportunities or lost crucial battles simply because of how we started...so while finishing is the ultimate goal how we start is just as important a goal...after all a good start gives us the JUMP on the week when others are still sleep...the JUICE to keep going strong when sometimes things go wrong...and the JOY in knowing that in the end we win..

~ *Dr. Ronald Thornhill*

www.ingramcontent.com/pod-product-compliance
Lightning Source LLC
Chambersburg PA
CBHW050657160426
43194CB00010B/1975